Auto-Movement for Beginners

Pendulums, Divining Rods, Glossolalia, Automatic Writing, Obsession and more …

Contact: www.HarryEilenstein.de
Harry.Eilenstein@web.de
Harry Eilenstein at youtube

Production and publishing: BoD - Books on Demand, Norderstedt

ISBN: 9783753454283

Table of Contents

I What is Auto-Movement?

"Auto-Movement" is a term for automatic movements, i.e. for actions which are not consciously controlled. This does not mean reflexes or unconscious actions, but movements of the body which one "lets the body do" without directing them consciously.

This may sound quite strange and possibly seems to be an urgent case for intensive psychological treatment, but auto-movement is an important element in many forms of magic. It is found in scrying, dowsing, automatic writing, "speaking in tongues" ("glossolalia") and also in more advanced methods such as invocation or even in more undesirable phenomena such as possession. The execution of a hypnotic command also belongs to this group of phenomena.

The usual source of an action is a conscious decision – at least this seems to be the case at first sight. However, if one looks at the manipulation of people by politicians or vaudeville magicians, this is no longer quite so certain.

If one makes oneself moreover conscious, how unconsciously most processes in the own body run off, as for example the respiration, the digestion or the blood formation in the bone marrow, then it shows up that the not consciously decided movements are possibly even in the clear predominance in humans.

The consciousness is obviously not "the driver at the steering wheel of one's own car" to the extent one would like to commonly assume. This circumstance suggests to take a closer look at consciousness.

I 1. The forms of consciousness

There are at least five types of consciousness – which operate a meaningful division of labor with each other:

1. **Deep sleep consciousness** is like a white screen. It is without content, but "present". It is the basis of all other forms of consciousness – it is, so to speak, the white canvas on which a picture can then be painted, or silence in which a sound can then appear.

One can consider the deep sleep consciousness as a house.

2. **Dream-consciousness**, which is also called subconsciousness, is the totality of all information in a psyche. All perceptions and all memories are contained in this consciousness – including the feelings associated with them.

One can consider the subconsciousness as the archive in the house.

3. **The waking consciousness** contains all the contents of consciousness that are relevant to the momentary situation and therefore must be processed as quickly and effectively as possible so that one can decide on the most meaningful and effective action.

You can think of the waking consciousness as the office desk in the house. The subconscious mind always sends all the necessary information to this desk.

4. **Ecstasy consciousness** contains only one content of consciousness. This consciousness usually occurs only when there is one thing that seems existentially important. As a rule, these are things which are connected either with pleasure (e.g. sex) or with fear (e.g. panic). There is also, as a third possibility, the high concentration on only one thing in meditation.

The ecstasy consciousness can be thought of as the light of the desk lamp on the desk in the house, which illuminates the one important content of consciousness as brightly as possible.

5. **The collective subconsciousness** consists of the contents of consciousness of a whole family, clan, people, humanity or all living beings on earth. It is, so to speak, organically structured – from the small collective units such as the family to the large collective unit of all living beings on earth. The smaller units are elements of the larger units.

One can consider the collective subconsciousness as the city in which the house stands. There is a possibility from each house to contact any other house in that city or even the city as a whole. This would generally be called "telepathy". This kind of contacts run usually from archic to archiv.

- Finally one could still ask oneself whether there is a **total consciousness** which corresponds, so to speak, to the land on which this house and this city stand. With it, however, one would already come into the religious area which plays only a very subordinate role in this book.

These five forms of consciousness can be linked together, which is generally called "meditation". Depending on the form of linking, other meditative states arise. Since meditation is intentional and one can also be consciously aware only when the waking consciousness is involved, waking consciousness is part of all these meditative states.

The usual forms of meditation are:

waking consciousness + dream consciousness   = dream journey.
waking consciousness + deep sleep   = silent meditation
waking consciousness + ecstasy   = tantra, magic
waking consciousness + collective subconsciousness = telepathy, seership
waking consciousness + all four   = mandala meditations

In considering the various forms of auto-movement, this model of consciousness is, so to speak, the map on which one moves.

Each of the four "personal" modes of consciousness has a specific frequency:

deep sleep $\approx$ 3 Hz (2 - 4 Hz)
dream consciousness $\approx$ 6 Hz (4 - 8 Hz)
waking consciousness $\approx$ 12 Hz (8 - 16 Hz)
ecstasy $\approx$ 24 Hz (16 - 32 Hz)

Each consiousness-frequence is the octave of the prceding one. The frequence is halved or doubled.

One can imagine the processes during meditation as a tuning of two consciousness frequencies to each other. In a dream journey, for example, two vibrations of the waking consciousness would vibrate together with one vibration of the subconsciousness.

This connection can be clarified most simply by a diagram:

The coordination of the rhythms of consciousness in meditation

uncoordinated rhythm (normal consciousness)												
deep sleep												
dream												
waking												
ecstasy												

coordinated rhythm (meditation)										
deep sleep										
dream										
waking										
ecstasy										

I 2. The connections between several consciousnesses

The connection between the consciousness of person A and the consciousness of person B is telepathy. Of course, this word does not explain anything at first, but it is at least a common term for this kind of connection. Since a part of the phenomena of auto-movement takes place between several persons, telepathy is also an important part of these phenomena.

Another form of connection in auto-movement is hypnosis, in which the hypnotist determines what the hypnotized person does. In this case, the source of the automatic movement, i.e., more precisely, the "not self-consciously decided movement" is the hypnotist.

A usually non-obvious form of hypnosis is suggestion and dominance, which can be seen, among other things, in skillful conversation, through which a dominant person can get others to do what he wants. This is a case of auto-movement, in which the person often does not even realize that he is being manipulated.

In the case of mass hypnosis or mass suggestion, which occurs mainly in the political sphere and is very popular with dictators, this directing of people's thoughts, speech and actions is either not noticed by these people at all or only later – often when it is already far too late.

Finally, there is the case of the disintegrated psyche, in which individual parts take over the steering, whereby the waking consciousness is not even always aware of this. This includes panic attacks, addictive behavior, fits of rage, psychosis, schizophrenia and the like. Here, too, one can speak of auto-movement in so far as the behavior is no longer consciously controlled and often cannot be consciously controlled at all.

I 3. Auto-movement in magic

In magic, auto-movement is used in many ways. In scrying, dowsing, and automatic writing, one cooperates with the subconscious and lets it partially and temporarily control one's own body. Thus one can use telepathy and sometimes also telekinesis, which are both abilities of the subconscious.

To be more precise, one should say that telepathic perceptions are send from the subconscious into the waking consciousness. In the model of consciousness described at the beginning, the waking consciousness is the desk in the office, but the information all comes from the archive of the subconscious (both the perceptions and the memories) – including the telepathic perceptions. It would therefore be more accurate to say that the subconscious mind has access to the telepathic information, not the waking conscious mind.

In hypnosis, the hypnotist takes control of the hypnotized, which was once an important element in magic around 1950, but is hardly used today.

In sigil magic, a completely different form of auto-movement is found: through the wish sent out by this method, it is not a person who moves unconsciously-automatically, but the world, which "brings" the desired thing to the magician by "meaningful coincidence".

Still another completely different application of the auto-movement is the invocation. In this case a deity is invoked, with whom one identifies oneself and who one lets speak and act through oneself.

II The Intentional Auto-Movement

One can divide the phenomena of auto-movement into three clearly distinguishable groups:

- the intentional auto-movement (e.g. commuting)
- unintentional auto-movement (e.g. remote hypnosis)
- and the collective auto-movement (e.g. crop circles).

II 1. Pendulum

In commuting one holds a pendulum in the hand and lets it swing without consciously doing anything to make it swing.

You use the arm with which you write. You hold it bent at the elbow about the height of the neck in front of you and hold the string of the pendulum with your hand.

There are basically four ways for the pendulum to swing:

- circular clockwise
- circular counterclockwise
- back and forth
- left and right

Strictly speaking, of course, all movements of the pendulum are ellipses. The four forms of oscillation mentioned are merely the extreme forms of the ellipse. If both radii of the ellipse are equal, it becomes a circle, if one of the two radii of the ellipses becomes "0", it becomes a back and forth motion.

To be able to use the pendulum these four movements are aimed at. Swinging back and forth from the front left to the back right for example would also be a possibility of swinging, but it is not usually used as a possible response.

In order to use the pendulum, it must be programmed beforehand, so to speak, i.e. one must determine the meanings of the movements.

As meaningful meanings for the four possible "distinctive" movements the following can be suggested:

- yes
- no
- don't know
- unclear/nonsensical/unanswerable question

You can of course think of other meanings, but "yes" and "no" will probably be needed for each version.

Which movements you use for which answers is up to you. It is obvious to use two opposite movements for "yes" and "no" – either the two circle movements or the two line movements. But this can also be handled differently.

No special materials are needed for the pendulum. For years, every time I needed a pendulum, I hung my front door key on my headband. But again, you should use what feels good. If a rock crystal on a silver chain feels better to you personally, you should also use such a pendulum.

The next point is asking meaningful questions – and exploring what questions the pendulum can answer at all.

It's a good idea to start by asking simple questions like "Am I a woman?", "Is it daytime?", "Do I have two hands?", etc. This way you can see if the pendulum gives the right answers, i.e. if the "programming" of the pendulum has worked.

So you hold the pendulum in front of you and ask the question. Then you do nothing and wait. At first, the pendulum will probably only wobble a little, but gradually the movements will become more distinct. Until you have achieved clear movements, you should first continue with simple questions – although humorous questions can certainly increase success: "Do I like raspberry ice cream?", "Does X love Y?", "Am I too fat?" and the like.

It can also be helpful to conduct these experiments in pairs, with one taking turns asking the other a question.

When the pendulum movements have become clear, one can go one step further and ask questions to which one does not know the answer, but where one can easily find out the answer.

If there are two of you, Person A can ask Person B, for example, the Hobbit-question "What do I have in my pocket?" Person B then has to start asking questions like "Is it round?", "Is it made of metal?", "Is it precious?", "Is it white?" etc. In this way, the answers given by the pendulum of Person B gradually create a clearer and clearer outline of the object in the pocket of person A. It is helpful, of course, if you enjoyed playing the question game as a child, where you have to guess what the other person is thinking about with the help of such questions and yes/no answers. By this procedure person B will see if his telepathy and his pendulum works well.

Next, you can move on to asking questions about things that no-one in the room knows, but that you can check. This type of question includes, for example, "How many coins does X have in his wallet?", "How many cars are in the parking garage?" or "How many phone calls will I receive today?" By this kind of questions it can be proved that "by pendulum" one can use telepathy (how-many coins, how-many cars) and likewise can foresee the future (number of calls).

When this kind of questions has been practiced, one can also ask more complex questions to which one does not know the answer, such as "What medicine will help me?", "What can I do about my lovesickness?" or "What job should I take?"

It is obvious that one should thoroughly examine the information received in this way on such existential questions – otherwise there is a danger of making oneself a puppet of one's pendulum.

The fact that the pendulum has access to telepathy and to foreseeing the future does not mean that the pendulum is omniscient or even that it is wise. This fact only means that the pendulum is a good telepathic aid.

Now, who is the one who gives the answers during the pendulum? It is certainly not the pendulum itself – but who else?

How does the movement of the pendulum come about? Obviously by the movements of the arm muscles. So there seems to be an instance which is able to control the movements of the arm muscles in such a way that meaningful pendulum movements and thus also meaningful answers result from it. This instance can only be the subconscious, which also contains the entire information of the psyche and which e.g. also controls largely autonomously complex, unconscious muscle movements when walking, speaking or knitting.

The pendulum is therefore a "monitor" for the subconscious, on which the opinion of the subconscious to the posed question is shown by the pendulum movements.

In the house-picture for the consciousness the pendulum is thus in the office (waking consciousness) – as a monitor on a side table next to the door that leads into the archive (subconsciousness). The waking consciousness at the office table can, if it wishes, request information from the archive with the help of the pendulum-monitor.

However, the waking consciousness should know what it is that is displayed on this monitor: There is no wise old woman or wise old man sitting in the archive, but rather a more or less neutral archivist who sends the information from the archive to the office of the waking consciousness in the same way as this information is present in the archive.

However, depending on the question the waking consciousness has used, this information may contain errors and be also incomplete. For example, if one has asked "Does chamomile help better than peppermint?" it may be that chamomile would be better than peppermint, but that actually comfrey is needed.

Another source of error is the feelings that might be associated with a piece of information from the archive. For example, if one asks "Why do I have abdominal pain?" the waking consciousness may not be able to hear the actual answer, "Because you were raped as a teenager." and instead, with the help of the pendulum, only finds out that you ate too much – which is only 2% of the cause of the abdominal pain.

So you should be careful with the information you receive "by pendulum" – and in no case let the pendulum direct your life. This direction should always remain with the waking consciousness.

II 2. Divining rod

The divining rod is a "Y"-shaped hazel branch, i.e. a branch fork. Sometimes a willow branch is used and in more recent times there are also metal dowsing rods. This branch or metal divining rod should not be rigid, but elastic.

It is held at the two ends, i.e. at the two branches of the branch fork with one hand each. The two branches are bent slightly apart so that the arm muscles are tense and the two branches are under tension. As a result, the arm muscles begin to tremble slightly – similar to bioenergetics exercises.

Due to this pressure and these uncontrolled arm movements, the lower branch (i.e. not the two branches of the branch fork) starts to "swing" upwards or downwards, which then gives the information – this corresponds to the "yes" and the "no" with the pendulum.

Traditionally, the dowsing rod is used to find things "under the ground" such as water veins, power cables, sewer pipes, buried treasures, and the like. This finding of material things under the ground is a combination of the telepathic abilities of the subconscious mind with the use of the dowsing rod as a monitor for the subconscious mind.

It is also used to examine the life force body of the earth, i.e., to detect power places, leylines (lines of life force), the grids (patterns in the life force of the earth), etc. Since the life force body of the earth is being examined here, a verification of these events of "dowsing" is not so easy at first.

However, if it has been shown by searching for power cables, buried treasures, etc., that a dowser can actually find things hidden in the earth with his dowsing rod, it has at least already been proven that the dowsing rod is a useful monitor for the telepathic abilities of the subconscious mind. If it is also shown that the information about the life force body obtained with the dowsing rod helps to solve problems such as sleep disorders or depressions, it can at least be said that the dowsing rod is also useful for this purpose.

There is no indication that the dowsing rod is anything other than a variant of the pendulum: the dowsing rod deflects upward or downward because the arm muscles, controlled by the subconscious mind, make slight movements that result in these movements of the dowsing rod.

Both the pendulum and the dowsing rod merely magnify the small movements of the arm, making them more visible.

II 3.   Finger monitor

The pendulum is very practical – but also very conspicuous. What should you do, for example, if you are sitting in a conference and want to ask the pendulum whether Mr. Maier is lying through his teeth? To unpack the pendulum and to swing it at the conference table is a bit too conspicuous …

After I had experienced such a situation once, I have thought that one should be able to use other things than only the pendulum or the divining rod as a monitor for the telepathic abilities of the subconsciousness. For the described situation this would have to be a monitor as inconspicuous as possible.

Since the pendulum is moved by the muscles in my arm, hand and fingers, I decided to use my fingers as a monitor. To do this, I placed my left forearm on the table in front of me and then placed my right hand over my left forearm so that the fingers of my right hand hung freely in the air.

Then I asked my right hand, "Which finger movement should mean 'yes'?" After a while, my index finger moved up and down a little automatically, that is, without my doing anything. This movement looked a bit funny – like a severely slowed nervous twitch. But it was inconspicuous enough to be "conference-worthy" as well.

Then I asked the remaining three fingers whose movement should mean "no", "don't know" and "unclear question".

With this "programming" I could now ask my subconscious completely unobtrusively and even without looking at my hand – after all, you can feel which finger you are moving, i.e. which finger is moving "by itself" even if you are not looking.

As with all these methods, it is also important with the finger monitor not to simply believe the results, but to regard them as an important indication and to check them as well as possible.

After all, you never know if the information arrived without interference – there could have been fears interfering in the subconscious, or hidden desires, there could have been interference due to lack of concentration, a very dominant person in the room could have clouded the perception, you could have been inattentive in some way, you could have not asked the question clearly enough, and so on.

One should take the information obtained "by pendulum", "by divining rod" or "by finger monitor" seriously, but never forget that they are telepathic perceptions and not optical perceptions with the eyes. This does not mean that telepathy is not precise, but like all things it requires practice – in this case to be able to distinguish telepathic perception from all associations and other disturbances, and also to acquire the necessary concentration.

II 4.   Automatic writing

Automatic writing is very similar to the finger monitor. You take a sheet of paper, put it in front of you on the table, take a pen that is as easy to write with as possible (i.e. not a pencil with a hard lead or an almost empty ballpoint pen) and hold it on the paper.

Now you ask a question and tell your arm and hand to write an answer. Then you wait and see what happens.

If you have already practiced with the pendulum and the finger monitor, you already know the neutral, "empty" posture that is helpful for this. Finally, the hand begins to move and scribble something on the paper.

At first, these will not yet be poetic sentences, but simply strokes. With practice, however, the subconscious learns to couple the brain department for writing with the brain department for arm movements and to direct both.

After some time, letters, words, sentences, and eventually interesting answers to the questions posed will emerge.

It is easier in most cases to learn automatic writing in pairs or threes – the kind of cheerful laughter that ensues over the scribbles generally seems to encourage all automatic processes and also all kinds of telepathy.

It is also possible that after some time one knows what the hand is about to write before it has begun to move – possibly one hears the words inwardly before the words appear on the paper. In these two cases the subconscious has simply chosen the waking consciousness or the sense of hearing as monitor – because these have been more easily accessible in with that person.

Of course, one can also use automatic writing to make drawings and possibly even to paint pictures. This is of course a bit more demanding than automatic writing – especially if different colored pencils are used.

Automatic writing has a big advantage over the pendulum, the divining rod and the finger monitor: The three aids mentioned can only answer with "yes" and "no", so that in many cases you have to ask a whole series of questions in a creative way and with a lot of skill to get useful answers. Automatic writing, however, can (with some practice) provide direct, sophisticated, and qualitative answers.

But again, while taking all the information obtained through automatic writing seriously (otherwise you might as well not do automatic writing at all), do not simply believe it (because otherwise you would become a chessman of your own subconscious mind).

II 5. Body monitor

Now that the arm, hand and finger muscles have become a capable monitor for the subconscious, it is obvious to expand this monitor further and see what happens – at least if you are a curious person and want to get to know yourself and your own possibilities.

First you can try to tell the arm and the hand to make a certain movement. Then you wait and watch what happens.

Next, you can extend the monitor function to the legs. To do this, you sit on a chair and put your right leg over your left leg. Then you simply tell the right leg to "move" and see what happens. Probably the perception of your own leg moving without your own conscious impulse still takes some getting used to …

The same can be done with the other leg.

You can also lie on your back, pull up your legs a bit so that your feet come closer to your butt and then ask both legs to move. There are no limits to creativity here.

You could also use these leg movements as a monitor – but this is quite impractical for everyday use …

Next comes the head's turn. This is a particularly strange experience, because most people locate their personality in the head and can look at the pendulum, the divining rod, the finger monitor and the automatic leg movements still distantly "from above". However, when the head automatically moves, nods, turns, circles, etc., then this experiment probably begins to question one's own ideas about one's own psyche: Where and what am I when my body, including my head, can move "by itself"?

Well, since you probably don't want to stop halfway as a rule, you can sit down on a chair and tell your own body to stand up. The experience of standing up without consciously directing it is indescribable….

Next, you can tell your body to walk a few steps or to grab something.

The automatic, i.e. not consciously controlled movements of the body are quite different from normal – jerky, angular, sudden, they seem awkward, but they are completely unerring … it has a little bit of a well-programmed robot …

The first time I did this experiment with my friend Jörg and told my body to touch Jörgs shoulder with my hand, he shook because it felt so creepy and said, "Only zombies are creepier!"

You can clearly see that in this experiment a body is moving without the normal consciousness. It appears as if the subconscious mind can calculate and perform the movements very precisely, but performs them gradually – which then creates this strange "robot effect".

Apparently the waking consciousness has the task to combine the different partial movements to a "soft" total movement. But the waking consciousness also brings doubts into the movements, which also makes the conscious movements somewhat less precise than the movements in the "zombie mode".

A better known version of "automatic body movement" ist sleepwalking.

II 6. Automatic speech

If these experiments are not already enough for you, there is another possibility: You tell your body to say something.

Possibly at first only sounds and tones come out of the mouth and a while later maybe the first words. It can take a while until you have installed your mouth as a "language monitor" for your subconscious.

The voice sounds "flat" and has almost no intonation – this apparently corresponds to the jerky, robot-like movements of the body when moving automatically.

The words also seem to tumble out of the mouth one after the other – you don't get the feeling that this is a sentence, although it is clearly a sentence in terms of grammar and words. It sounds a bit like an old-fashioned computer, which simply emits words one after the other through its loudspeaker, but does not yet have a program that regulates the emphasis of the words and the speech melody. This apparently also corresponds to the jerky, successive movements in the "zombie mode", in which each movement is separate.

The brevity of the sentences in automatic speech corresponds to the precision of the movements of the body in automatic movements.

It is important not to allow these automatic movements to be a constant possibility, but to control this "zombie mode" and "turn it on" only when needed for something – otherwise you may find yourself suddenly in an uncomfortable situation.

II 7. Body-"messenger"

As a monitor, the "zombie mode" is quite useless: one step forward as "yes" and one step back as "no" would be very awkward – the finger monitor is much more elegant.

But if the whole body can move automatically, you can also give the body an order and send it out as a messenger to fulfill this order. In general, of course, there is nothing that you can't do far better consciously with your own body – putting on your shoes, clearing the table, combing your hair, and so on. You can try these things in the "automatic version" for fun (and amuse yourself with the "zombie version" of combing your hair), but it is not really useful.

However, since the subconscious mind has telepathic abilities, there are quite interesting application possibilities for automatic moving. I have tried these possibilities together with my son David.

After I had practiced automatic moving with him until it was fluent (which took us about 10 minutes), I told him that I had hidden a ring in my room which he should now look for. So he sat down on a chair and told his body to look for the ring.

Then his front body folded forward, he bent his knees, which made his head point downward, and finally he straightened his upper body. Apparently, his subconscious calculated the most energy-saving variant for standing up and then performed the standing up in these three movements. This looks rather robotic and on the other hand, as a spectator, one wonders whether the person in question will not fall over immediately, because the type of movement looks so mechanical.

Then David took two "stilted" steps forward, turned 90° to the right and took three more steps.

Then came a very strange movement, which on the one hand was very fluid and precise, and on the other hand looked like falling over – and of course again mechanical-robotic: David dropped his upper body forward and stretched out his arm, causing his hand to "bump" under the edge of the carpet; then he immediately came back up and held the ring in his hand, which I had hidden right there under the carpet.

We were both quite amazed at the success of this experiment …

A few months later, David developed problems with the meniscus in both knees and had to walk on crutches and was to have surgery on both knees. When he was on the school graduation trip in Nuremberg at the top of the castle shortly before the operation and was the last of the class to stand in the castle courtyard, he remembered our experiment with the hidden ring.

There he said to his body that he should do what heals his knees again. That's when his body went to a door at the edge of the castle courtyard that David hadn't noticed before. His body opened the door, which had not been locked. Then David saw before him a bed of herbs high up on the battlements of the castle wall. His body stalked unerringly to the last bed. There he bent forward again with such a strange flowing motion, tore off a piece of an herb, put it in his mouth and swallowed it … and was quite stunned at what had just happened.

That's when he tried out how his knees were doing – all pain was gone! Then he put his crutches under his arm and from then on he didn't need them anymore and was able to do sports again as before (he is a parcour trainer and ninja warrior).

The "sending out of ons's body" is obviously very useful, because the body can then do the things it needs guided by the subconscious.

Of course, there is also the possibility of simply having this information sent to the waking consciousness as an inner voice or intuition and then consciously carrying it out. However, a well-trained neutrality of the waking consciousness is necessary in order not to interfere in the perception of this information and in the execution of these instructions.

In view of these many possibilities, one should always consider which method of auto-movement will achieve one's goal with the least effort.

II 8.   Finger signal

In general, it is advisable to use the automatic mode of the musculature only on special decision and, in general, to always move consciously.

As with almost everything, however, there is an exception to this rule, where one does not consciously switch on the automatic mode oneself out of control, but rather generally releases this mode for special situations.

When I was about 25 years old, I struggled with myself quite a bit – and then I ran almost always into a lamppost, a tree or something similar and lay on the ground with a bruise and a pretty bad headache.

At some point I noticed the connection between these accidents and the feeling of self-rejection, self-contempt and self-hatred just before these accidents. A very similar scene of self-punishment is meanwhile well known from the "Harry Potter" books by the house elf Dobby …

There I got the idea to ask my body that every time I thought something unkind about myself, to let my right hand bump very lightly somewhere. In return, I promised my body that every time I lightly bumped my right hand somewhere, I would stop and see what I had just been thinking and feeling.

Since then, I have had no more unpleasant, sudden encounters with lampposts …

II 9.   The memory messenger

When I was young, it bothered me that sometimes I couldn't remember a thing. So I looked to see what would help my memory.

Searching for hours in my memory almost never helped.

19

If I was only looking for a single word, I slowly spoke the alphabet inwardly and looked at each letter to see if the word I was looking for began with that letter – this helped with single words in most cases, but not always either.

Finally, I noticed that the memory I was looking for often came when I had given up trying to find it (which usually took quite a long time). So I tried to see if the memory would come by itself when I wasn't looking for it. However, that didn't work either.

However, if I concentrated briefly but intensively on the memory I was looking for and then did something completely different that took up all my attention, the memory suddenly came.

From this I derived the image of a messenger that I create by concentrating on the missing memory and then send off – and which I should not disturb, if possible, by thinking about that memory.

This "memory messenger" is also an automated process, which, however, does not take place in the body, but in the consciousness. Also the monitor of this process is not a part of the body, but the consciousness itself.

This discovery was the beginning of the image of the waking consciousness as a desk in an office and the subconscious as an archive in the same house as this office. I could obviously send an "office messenger" to the archive to get the information I needed – if I did not disturb the "office messenger" in his work, but occupied myself with something else in the time until his return.

A very practical matter – especially when with increasing age the short-term memory is not quite as good as it once was …

II 10. Dream journeys

During a dream journey one is simultaneously in the waking consciousness and in the dream consciousness (subconsciousness). This is the state in which one is in the morning directly after waking up, when the last dream continues to run in its own momentum for another 10 seconds and one can consciously watch it like a film. Also the vivid daydream of the last vacation, when one sits bored in the train, is such a dream journey.

With a little practice, one can also perform such dream journeys consciously – that is, have intentional and conscious daydreams, so to speak.

By defining before such a dream journey what you want to see something about, you can find out something about the subject in question – both information from your subconscious mind and telepathically procured "external information" from other people, places and times.

This defining of the theme of a dream journey may be a word you say inwardly ("the element fire"), a greeting to the thing you want to know something obout („Hello beech-tree!") or a picture, through which you go as if it were a door ("the symbol of Saturn").

With the dream journey, one no longer sends the office messenger to the archive to look for the information there, but one goes to the archive oneself to look around in the department in question. The advantage of the dream journey compared to sending the office messenger is obvious: you receive much more information of the surroundings of the theme in question and also more detailed information about this theme.

In terms of detail, automatic writing and automatic drawing lie between sending the office messenger (commuting, dowsing, etc.) and going to the archive yourself (dream journey).

Also the things one experiences on a dream journey should be taken seriously, but one should not simply believe them, but look at them carefully and ask oneself in what way one wants to use this information.

II 11. **Inner listening**

If you do dream journeys often, you will notice that you can use different senses as an "inner monitor". In some dream journeys one sees mainly pictures, in others one hears mainly words, in still others the sense of touch, the sense of smell and the sense of warmth also play a role.

With enough practice, you can determine beforehand what type of dream journey you want to take:

- If one begins the dream journey with a question to a deity, for example, the dream journey will become primarily a conversation.

- If you start the dream journey by going through a door on which you have written your question or drawn a symbol of what you want to learn about, you will mainly see pictures.

Of course, during the dream journey itself, one can direct one's attention more to images or mote to words or more to smells, etc.

21

It is also possible to make the hearing of words on the dream journey independent and to use it as a small auxiliary element in everyday life and simply to direct a question inwardly to one's own subconscious or even to a deity and then listen to what comes as an answer.

II 12. Glossolalia

Glossolalia or "speaking in tongues" is a special form of automatic speaking. The special thing about this variant is that one speaks in languages which one has never learned and which one has possibly never heard.

In some cases the glossolalia comes over the person unexpectedly, in other cases this "speaking in foreign tongues" can be caused consciously.

Sometimes the language used can be identified, but sometimes it cannot (then you don't know if it's a real language …).

There are enough documented cases where a person could suddenly speak a foreign language without having learned it. This does not only concern closely related languages, but also completely foreign languages, such as the English woman who suddenly can speak Chinese.

Apparently, in the glossolalia, the subconscious mind has telepathically "logged in" to the collective subconscious mind of the people whose language it can suddenly speak.

As far as I know, the "learning" of glossolalia has almost always happened in a spontaneous way unconsciously and unintentionally – but there is actually no reason to believe that this should not be possible consciously.

In glossolalia, the collective subconsciousness of the people whose language is spoken in glossolalia is added to the waking consciousness as an essential element.

In glossolalia, the automatic movement takes place in the throat and in the mouth, which form the words that are unknown to the waking consciousness.

The most famous case of glossolalia in Western culture is probably the speaking of the apostles at Pentecost in various languages they had never learned.

II 13.   The Understanding of foreign languages

Understanding foreign languages is much more common than speaking foreign languages – sometimes you just know exactly what someone else in a foreign country is saying, even if you don't know the language. Sometimes you hear the foreign language as if it had been simultaneously translated into your own mother tongue, sometimes you see the meaning of the words as images.

I myself have experienced this several times and know several people who know this strange phenomenon. This can be very practical during vacations in foreign countries …

II 14.   Telekinesis

Telepathy is not the only connection the subconscious has "to the outside". Besides the "direct external perception" by the consciousness, there is also the "direct external effect" by the consciousness, i.e. telekinesis.

Since the different forms of auto-movement refer to the transition between the waking consciousness and the subconsciousness, i.e. to the "door" between the "office" and the "archive", one should be able to assume that a closer look at telekinetic phenomena will make the essence of auto-movement even clearer.

II 14. a)   Smilie experiment

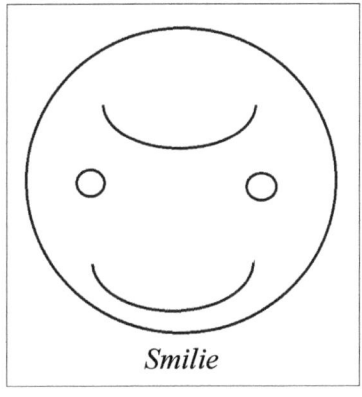

Smilie

For the "smilie experiment" one needs a sheet of paper on which the "smilie" shown on the left is drawn. This sheet with the drawing is placed at the edge of a table in such a way that a person standing in front of the table sees this picture as shown on the left.

Now person A stands in front of the table and spreads his arms to the left and right like a "T", i.e. like a cross. Person A should keep his arms in this posture as much as possible during the following trials and not change them.

Person B stands behind A and places his right hand on A's right elbow and his left hand on A's left elbow.

A looks at the smilie and B presses on A's elbows. Nothing happens – B can lean on A's elbows and B can rise his feet even in the air.

Now the smilie is turned over (see the illustration on the left) and the experiment is repeated in the same way – and A's arms fold down powerlessly. A is unable to keep his arms sideways.

umgedrehtes Smilie

What happened here? Obviously, looking at the picture has a greater effect on A than A's conscious decision to keep his arms up.

Two kinds of effect are possible:

- First, the "depressed smilie" could suggest to A that he is now failing in his attempt to keep his arms up.

- On the other hand, the two "Ո" of the mouth and the forehead crease of the smilie A could suggest that he should drop his arms, so that they then have the same posture together with his shoulders as the "Ո".

This experiment shows that the subconsciousness also reacts to external information and not only to the decision in the waking consciousness. Obviously, the impression that the sight of the "Ո" makes on the subconscious is much greater than the decision to keep the arms up.

The concentration on the "Ո"-smilie by the waking consciousness in the "office" (A looks at the smilie during the experiment) obviously sends the "office messenger" with the message into the "archive" that the "Ո"-state should be reached.

This experiment shows clearly what suggestions, advertising, demagogy and the like can be capable of when one no longer consciously controls what one's own waking consciousness concentrates on.

II 14. b)   Dragon claw experiment

There are many variations of the smilie experiment, one of which is the "dragon claw experiment";

A stands upright and extends his right arm straight out in front of him – palm up. B stretches his own right arm straight towards him – palm down.
B puts his hand on A's hand and tries to push A's arm down – in vain.

Then B raises his right arm in the air and stretches his index finger upward, imagining that his index finger is a dragon's claw. Then he presses A lightly with his index finger on the spot between the eyebrows ("Third Eye").
Now A and B hold their outstretched arms as before – and B pushes A's arm down effortlessly.

Again, there are two possible explanations:

> - The raising of the arm by B and his pointing upward with his index finger is a gesture of greatness, which is understood and accepted by A's subconscious as B's dominance over A. The same can be said of B's pushing down A's arm.

> - The pressure on the Third Eye of A is understood and accepted by it as submission of A under B – in the Third Eye lies the will, the orientation in the world, one's own goals. Possibly this slight pressure on the Third Eye temporarily turns off A's will, i.e. he unconsciously gives up his resistance to B's pushing down A's arm.

II 14. c)   Shaolin experiment

For the "Shaolin experiment" a table top, a fence post or something similar is used, which has a smooth surface at a height of about 1.20m.
Person A places his left fist on this surface. Person B and person C grab A's wrist and fist and hold them on to the surface.
Now A looks at his fist, which is held by B and C, and tries to pull it away – in vain …

25

Now the experimental arrangement is changed: A turns away from B and C and looks into his right palm, which he holds in front of his eyes with a slightly bent arm at a distance of about 40cm – and simply walks away, pulling B and C behind him.

In this experiment, the gesture that makes the difference is looking into his own hand and "not caring about the two persons holding one's fist".
Here again there are two possible interpretations:

- B and C lose strength because they see that A does not care about them.

- A gains strength because he does not care about B and C.

First of all, there is no possibility to choose one of the two interpretations as the correct description.
However, it is worth noting that here one of the interpretation variants suggests that A has become stronger and not B and C weaker. One could also interpret the two previous attempts ("smilie" and "dragon's claw") in such a way that B has become stronger – but this is unlikely, at least in the "smilie experiment", since there A concentrates on the smilie and B does nothing special.

II 14. d) "Hepp" experiment

"Hepp" is a german word which signifies "Come on!", "Jump", "Now!", and the like.

Person A lies down with his belly on the ground and puts his arms next to his body or next to his head. Person B lies down with her belly across the calves of person A. Both persons together now look approximately like a "T".
Person A now tries to lift person B up with his legs – which usually will not be possible. Person A should take care of her legs and not get a muscle strain by doggedly overexerting herself.
Then person A imagines that from her head to her feet flows a white ray of light, which splits into two rays in her buttocks. Then person A imagines that person B is just a small pillow, light as a feather cloud. Now person A inwardly says "Hepp!" and at the same time lifts person B with his calves – and person B will in all probability roll over person A's back with some momentum …
Here clearly A is the active person. Since she cannot reduce the real weight of B, something else must happen here. There are two interpretations for this:

26

- A increases his power. The question would arise how he can be able to do this.

- A uses telekinesis, i.e. he instructs his subconscious by the images imagined by him to lift up telekinetically person B who is lying on his calves.
Provided that one has already experienced telekinesis, this is the more probable interpretation.

There are some cases with many eyewitnesses where a person has lifted an object so heavy that normally this would have been completely impossible for him. Such a case is, for example, the mother lifting a truck in order to free her child who is half under one of the wheels of the truck.

If we assume telekinesis as a possible explanation, telekinesis could also be involved in the previous attempts. However, the first two attempts ("Smilie" and "Dragon Claw") can be explained well without telekinesis. Only the Sholin experiment could also be explained by telekinesis.

II 14. e) Chair experiment

There is a simple levitation experiment. For this experiment five persons and one chair are needed.

One person sits on a chair, the other four stand around him. The four people hold their hands horizontally with the palms down, clench their fingers into two fists and then extend only the two index fingers forward – the two fngers touching each other along their entire length.

Then the four standing people put their index fingers under the two armpits and under the two knees of the seated person and try to lift him up – which will most likely not succeed.

Next, the four standing people place their hands on top of each other on the sitter's head and sing a note together – simply an "a" at any pitch.

Now the lifting of the sitter is repeated with the help of the index fingers – which now succeeds effortlessly, since the sitter no longer seems to have any weight.

The easiest way to explain this phenomenon is telekinesis – the four "lifters" have not suddenly become stronger, nor do they feel much pressure on their two index fingers at the armpits and the back of the knees of the "sitter". The lifting is quite easy …

One could also call the effect of this experiment "levitation", but what is levitation other than telekinesis, which is used for levitating things and people?

Thus there are now already three experiments in which the participation of telekinesis is very probable (Shaolin experiment, Hepp experiment and Chair experiment).

II 14. f) Paper wheel experiment

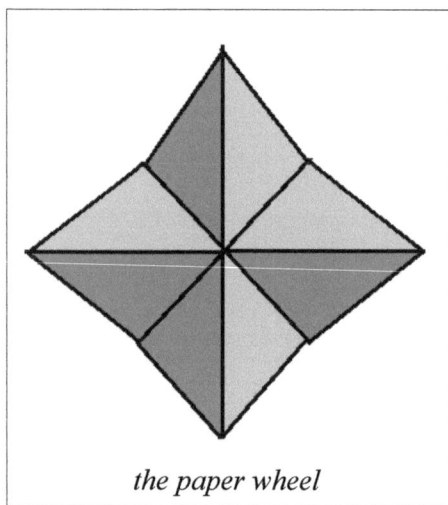

the paper wheel

There is an experiment with which one can prove telekinesis directly. You can find it at "youtube" under the keyword "psi-wheel". However, it is useful to perform the experiment yourself, so that you can experience that it really works.

In this experiment you put a pin through a piece of cardboard and place both on a table with the tip of the pin pointing upwards.

Then fold a piece of paper of the size of 3,5cm x 3,5cm, so that it looks at the end like in the picture on the left. Then place the center of the paper wheel on the tip of the needle so that it lies still and can be turned with very little effort.

Finally, hold your hands next to the paper wheel and imagine that you are turning the paper wheel.

This experiment can only be explained by telekinesis.

These experiments require an extended picture of the "office messenger" and its possibilities:

- The office messenger can fetch information from the archive, i.e. from the subconscious, for the waking consciousness at the desk in his office.
This is an "internal process".

- The office messenger can request information from other houses of the city in the archive by telepathy and then bring it to the office.

In doing so, he uses the collective subconsciousness that connects all the "houses" with telepathic "telephone lines".

This is an "external process".

- The office messenger follows not only the conscious instructions of the waking consciousness in the office, but also the information on which the waking consciousness concentrates – information on which the waking consciousness concentrates either by its own decision, by the manipulation of others or possibly also accidentally and incidentally.

This is an "internal/external process."

- The office messenger can also order a telekinetic action in the archive, if the office messenger receives a clear order from the office for it.

This is also an "external process".

II 14. g)   Sigill-Magic

In sigil magic, talismanic magic, invocations and some other forms of magic by which the magician wants to bring about the fulfillment of a wish, he concentrates on an image that represents the fulfilled wish. This can be a sigil, a planetary symbol, a drawing, an imagined picture, etc.

This image, created in the office of the waking consciousness, is then brought to the archive by the office messenger. From this point on, the magician should not disturb the office messenger – this is the same situation as the office messenger retrieving a forgotten memory from the archive of the subconscious mind.

The office messenger now sends out of the archive telepathic messages and possibly also telekinetic impulses, which by means of the collective subconsciousness reaches the people and things that can fulfill the magician's wish. The result of these telepathic and telekinetic actions of the office messenger in the archive is then the "meaningful coincidence" which fulfills the wish of the magician.

II 14. h) Wishes

However, the office messenger does not have to be instructed with great effort what to do – it is enough to make a "wish en passant" which is not even thought of afterwards. Such wishes tend to come true.

This connection is widespread – even if you think of something you don't want, this image of the undesirable tends to come true. This connection has given rise to the proverb "Speak of the devil …" and the principle of "positive thinking" is also based on it.

II 14. i) Arm experiment

In the arm experiment, person A sits at a table and person B sits next to it. A keeps his eyes closed (possibly cover his eyes with a bandage). Both put their right arm on the table.

Now B points to A with his left arm and his outstretched left index finger in a commanding gesture (a symbolic connection). If B then raises his arm, A will do the same, and if B lowers his arm, A will do the same – and this without A being able to see what B is doing.

This experiment is further evidence of telepathy. B's command gesture apparently has the effect of B sending the arm movement command to A, and A receiving and obeying that command.

This experiment makes the collective subconscious a little more vivid – A and B are apparently telepathically coupled to each other.

II 15. Invocation

"Invocation" means "calling in." This term refers to the calling in of a deity into the person who invokes that deity.

For example, every day the Jesuit monks read scenes from the New Testament that tell about Christ – but not from the point of view of a spectator, but from Christ's point of view. Through this kind of reading and meditation, the Jesuits identify with Jesus – and have therefore been named "Jesuits," or "Jesus-men."

In Tibetan Buddhism, monks identify with their guru and with various aspects of

Buddha.

The method is always similar, no matter among which people and in which religion invocations are performed: One imagines the figure of the deity as vividly as possible and then unites with that deity. In the West, one usually imagines the deity standing in front of oneself, in the East, the deity is usually floating above one's head.

This is a method of inner growth that is also popular with children, who often play at being a horse or a hero like Obi wan Kenobi from Star Wars.

Such identification can be rather superficial, but also very intense. I know a woman who used to get sores on her hands, feet, and stomach on Good Friday because she had been so closely associated with Christ.

Through identification with a role model, if this identification is intense enough, one can also adopt their attitude toward life and their abilities. This can also be experienced on a small scale if, while watching a movie, one puts oneself in the place of one of the characters in the movie and then remains in that character's body feeling and life feeling for a while after the movie ends.

Invoking a deity can lead to having the powers of that deity. For this, no formal identification through a circumstantial invocation is necessary: Christ, before performing a miracle, thanked God that he will let that miracle happen – he thanked god before the miracle, not afterwards. In Christ and Yahweh, the connection between the two has been constantly present through Christ's unwavering trust in God.

An important element in these invocations is the image of the one being invoked. He is also the image of what one wants to achieve. It is therefore the concentration on the goal – this corresponds to the sigil magic already described and also to the images that are sent into the subconsciousness through the "office messenger".

The invocation is therefore a pictorial message of the waking consciousness in its "office" to the archive of the subconsciousness, from where telepathic and telekinetic actions are then set in motion.

Since deities are not only images in the personal subconscious, but also in the collective subconscious, the effect of the imagination of a deity image is naturally especially great.

The creation of abilities through an image is also found in individual actions. For example, my son advises the young people who are learning Parcour and Ninja Warrior with him to first imagine a jump that is difficult for them while sitting down with their eyes closed until they can feel it in every detail. When they have achieved this, they can also perform this jump with their body.

In the end, this is nothing different from the Hepp experiment or the Shaolin experiment: one imagines an image which then makes the deed possible.

This is the way Master Yoda acts …

31

II 16. Oracle

There is another automatic movement, which at first is not noticeable as such: The choosing of a tarot card, the throwing of rune stones, the dividing of yarrow stalks in the I Ching etc.

In an oracle, one asks a question and then begins an action that leads to an answer to that question in the end. If one bases this process on the model used in this book, a simple course of events results:

- The waking consciousness in its "office" speaks the question.

- The "office messenger" brings the question to the "archive".

- From the "archive" the necessary information is telepathically obtained from the "city", i.e. from the collective subconscious: the answer to the question and also the order of the tarot cards in the deck lying before the person seeking advice.

- The "archive" controls which tarot cards the hands select.

- The "office", based on its knowledge of the tarot cards, interprets these cards as answers to the questions it has asked.

- The "archive" sends the "office" possibly furthermore some pictures and information as "intuition", which the "office" adds then to the interpretation. This process is, so to speak, a "semi-conscious and unplanned dream journey".

The aspect of auto-movement in this process is the drawing of the "right" tarot cards that contain the answer to the question asked.

II 17. Firewalk

In a firewalk, one walks barefoot over 700-800°C hot glowing coals. You can also hold the glowing charcoal in your hands, lie naked on the embers, or eat a piece of embers.

Fire walking is an extreme form of telekinesis, if you define the term "telekinesis" a bit broader as "influencing the normal properties and behavior of matter".

You can't really describe what you do when you do a firewalk, and you certainly can't explain how it works. One decides something and then carries it out. Again, with the help of the office messenger, the office sends an image to the archive that, by telekinesis, makes the body temporarily impervious to embers.

The office messenger is the essential actor in magic.

II 18. Power animal

The processes described so far, such as the scrying of the place where one left one's identity card, or the Shaolin experiment, are not isolated in the psyche – the archive is not a big chaos, but well-ordered.

One of the important images in the archive is the power animal, which represents one's way of doing things. Two other important images are the power plant, which illustrates one's posture, and the power stone, which shows the nature of one's inner structures.

So the office messenger does not enter a hall full of chaos when he comes out of the office and enters the archive. In the archive, as dream interpretation, dream journeys, hypnosis, psychology etc. show, is ordered by associations. Thus, the individual memories are combined into more complex images, i.e. into symbols. These symbols are in turn linked together to form the "main images" such as "mother", "danger", "sex", "food" and the like.

As telepathy shows, these "main-pictures" in the subconciousness like e.g. the picture of the mother, which exists in all people, are connected once again to the original pictures in the collective subconsciousness. These primordial images are the deities.

These images in the psyche and in the collective subconscious are not only completely passive "books in the shelves of the archive", but have a momentum of their own, which becomes apparent when one consciously makes contact, for example, with one's own power animal or with a deity.

The power animal has all the possibilities that the office messenger has – the power animal is a part of the archive. So you can also ask your own power animal to find something lost, or ask a deity to bring something desired into your life.

However, the power animal is more than just a part of one's archive – it forms an archetype together with all other power animals of the same kind in other people. These power animals also have a common mother – the mother goddess of that species.

In the inner images in the archive (personal subconscious) and in the city (collective subconscious) there are many connections …

For example, I once visited Frater U.D. in the Siebengebirge who had just moved. On the way there a screw on my bicycle loosened, which I wanted to tighten again for the return trip. Since Frater U.D. had just moved, he didn't know where the wrench might be in his new apartment. I then asked my wolf if she knew where the wrench was. She then showed me one of the drawers on a cupboard – where the wrench was actually lying.

If one connects the experiments described in the previous chapters of this book and the findings from these experiments (which have all been described in a rather sober and objective manner) with one's own power animal, these possibilities become much more vivid.

II 19. Integration

The automatic movements are not a goal in themselves. They merely make telepathy and telekinesis more accessible. Ultimately, of course, it is desirable to make both telepathy and telekinesis as conscious as possible, so that they become as natural as seeing with the eyes and acting with the hands. One then becomes capable of perception and action in the "realm of the life force".

> Through the ability to perceive in the "realm of the life force" one becomes a seer;

> Through the ability to act in the "realm of the life force" one becomes a magician.

III   The Unintentional Auto-Movement

So far, only those automatic movements have been considered which the one who performs them has willed. However, there are also a number of automatic movements that are not willed by the one who performs them.

III 1.   Sleepwalking

The best known unintentional automatic movement is sleepwalking. In this case, the sleeper usually goes to another place in the house where he lives. This phenomenon occurs in about 15% of children and in about 2.5% of adults – so it is not a rare phenomenon.

The state of sleepwalking lasts from a few minutes to an hour. Sleepwalkers often just keep walking straight ahead, running the risk of hitting a wall or falling down a flight of stairs. However, there are also sleepwalkers who are aware of their surroundings but continue to sleep anyway.

This state corresponds to hypnosis – in both cases the subject's body is controlled by his subconscious mind, while the waking consciousness is "switched off". Like most hypnotized people, many sleepwalkers are also responsive – however, one can only talk to the subject's subconscious mind. This can be seen, among other things, in the fact that sleepwalkers, like hypnotized people, do what they are told – e.g. return to bed. Among children this is sometimes used to send the sleepwalking brother or sister to a "funny place" like the bathtub …

"Talking in sleep" is a variant of sleepwalking, which usually occurs only for a maximum of one minute, during which one can ask the sleeping person questions, which he answers truthfully – like under hypnosis.

During sleepwalking and "sleep-talking" the subconscious mind takes over the control of the body, as it does with the many variants of automatic movements.

The movements of a sleepwalker also look similar to those in the experiments where one gives an order to one's own body and then watches how it carries out this order. However, the sleepwalker's movements look a little less hard – they seem more clumsy. Possibly this difference is due to the fact that the waking consciousness is present in the "auto-movement" attempts in contrast to the sleepwalkers (but is limited to the role of a spectator of what one's own body is doing).

35

III 2.   Hypnosis

In hypnosis, the waking consciousness of the hypnotized is "switched off" by words or gestures or stroking over the vital force body ("mesmerism"). In hypnosis, therefore, one can still talk to the subject and ask him to do certain things, but one has as a counterpart only the subconscious of the hypnotized and not his waking consciousness. Therefore, after waking up, i.e. after the return of their waking consciousness, the hypnotized usually do not know what they have said and done under hypnosis.

In hypnosis, the hypnotist determines what the hypnotized person does – the hypnotist, through his words, sends an "office messenger" into the "archive" of the hypnotized person, where the "office messenger" then carries out his order.

The words of the hypnotist are thus very similar to the effect of the smilie picture in the section "13. a)" in this book: Information comes from outside into the subconsciousness of the subject, which determines in which way the subconsciousness of the subject directs his own body – and if necessary also adds telepathy and telekinesis.

III 3.   Remote hypnosis

In remote hypnosis, one person is hypnotized by another, although both may be several miles apart. In remote hypnosis, hypnosis and telepathy have been combined.

In this process, the hypnotist telepathically sends information into the subconscious mind of the hypnotized person.

In the previous considerations, the subconscious has always used telepathy to obtain certain "external information" – with the exception of the arm experiment, in which person A controls person B's movements by gestures that person B cannot see. In remote hypnosis the hypnotist uses telepathy.

Telepathic hypnosis can also be performed with people who are in the same room: The hypnotist telepathically sends a command to this person, which he then carries out. If the hypnotist has practice, he can even "command" another person to think he is a dog and bite someone else's leg.

This form of hypnosis is well known from the "Star Wars" movies as the Jedi Knight's command gesture and from the "Harry Potter" books as the "Imperio!" spell. However, it takes a lot of will and concentration to be able to send out such a hypnotic command effectively.

The difference to normal telepathy, where a person suddenly "hears" the wish of another person and then brings him the desired apple from the cold buffet, differs from telepathic hypnosis in that in normal telepathy nobody imposes his own will on the other person.

As one can see, the consideration of all these "auto-movement" processes, in which in one way or another an automatic, not consciously controlled movement occurs, leads step by step to a better understanding of the division of labor between the different forms of consciousness in the psyche – and also to a better understanding of the possibilities of using this division of labor, as well as of the possibilities of disturbing the smooth running of this division of labor from the outside.

These insights finally lead to an improved chance to act independently and self-determined – through the improved understanding of the structure and processes in one's own psyche.

III 4. The unconscious invocation

The conscious variant of an invocation consists of wanting something and getting the help of a deity for it or asking this deity for it. In the house parable used in this book, the office messenger is sent from the office to the archive, from where he telepathically contacts the appropriate archetype (deity) in the city, which in turn sends the desired things and events to the house in which the office is located.

However, there is also the case that the waking consciousness wants to do something specific in its office, but does not yet have an exact plan how it could carry this out. In such a case, the desire to achieve something specific sends the office messenger, who then independently organizes the appropriate thing.

This suitable thing can be the contact to Pan, who then organizes a hot night for the person concerned; it can be the intuitive knowledge of a form of classical Indian dance, which one suddenly uses in a dance improvisation on stage without ever having learned it; it can be the ability to do a difficult parcour-jump, which one has never practiced before …

There are many possibilities and most of them will probably not be noticed at all. Since the waking consciousness has not called for a particular solution to its problem and has not decided to turn to someone else for help, such as a deity, the waking consciousness may only notice this outside help when, for example, one notices where Pan suddenly appears everywhere in one's life, or when one is asked where one learned Indian temple dance, or when one notices that one has just made a leap that always seemed completely out of reach.

The automatic movement or the "automatic event" almost always needs a conscious impulse, but this conscious impulse can also still be so vague and general that the waking consciousness does not even perceive this impulse as a wish, which is brought by the office messenger into the archive of the subconsciousness and from there then further into the city of the collective subconsciousness.

This can be experienced as a "lucky coincidence" – as soon as one has noticed more clearly that there is an intense wish in one, the fulfillment of the wish comes. In the example of the dance improvisation, the dancer may not even be aware that she is dancing Indian dance – she just sensed the quality of the situation and followed the movements that felt right …

III 5. Stigmata

Probably no one will want to have stigmata on purpose, that is, Christ's wounds when He hung on the cross – because these stigmara, that is, these bleeding wounds on the hands and feet (from the nails of the cross) as well as on the abdomen (from the spear) can be downright painful and obstructive.

However, since these wounds belong to the "mythology of Christ", there is a possibility that the archive believes that it is supposed to produce these wounds when the office messenger keeps bringing the image of Christ to the archive from the office, because the person keeps focusing on Christ.

This process is ultimately nothing other than the smilie experiment: one sends an image to the archive via office messenger, which then triggers an effect there. This sending does not have to be a conscious sending and this sending does not have to be connected with the knowledge about the consequences of this sending – it is enough that the waking consciousness concentrates to a sufficient degree on the picture in question.

At this point the desk lamp on the desk in the office comes into play, symbolizing the ecstasy state. The ecstasy state is essentially one-pointedness – the desk lamp shines a spotlight on what is most important at the moment.

For example, if one repeatedly meditates on Christ and experiences Christ as the essential thing in the world, then the office messenger will bring this image to the archive with a great urgency, which naturally leads to correspondingly intense reactions there – such as, in this case, possibly the formation of stigmata.

This process exists also in the everyday life: If one goes at night by the forest and suddenly a big dog comes running, one will concentrate also completely on this dog, whereby the office messenger brings this picture into the archive, whereupon there immediately all possible ways of reaction are picked out and are sent then by office messenger into the office, where then one of these possibilities of action is selected.

In addition, from the archive probably also the adrenalin production is ramped up, so that a fast physical reaction becomes possible.

III 6. Repetition compulsion

The connection described in the previous section is an essential part of the repetition compulsion, which is well known from psychology: people always get into the same situation and experience the same thing again and again.

On the one hand, this is due to the horoscope of the person concerned, which brings certain themes to the fore. But since one can live each theme at very different levels, one cannot reduce the repetition compulsion to the horoscope.

For example a square (separation) between Pluto (essence) and Saturn (form) can be lived in many different ways: As a criminal who does what he wants (Pluto) and does not care about laws (Saturn); as a prisoner in a jail (Saturn) where he is subject to laws (Saturn) but cannot do what he wants (Pluto); as a social critic who opposes what he wants (Pluto) to conditions as they are (Saturn); as a magician who does what he wants (Pluto) and does not care about the laws of nature (Saturn); etc.

The decision of how a person lives his horoscope lies with that person, with his waking consciousness.

The repetition compulsion arises in a very simple way:

For example, if a person has been abandoned as a child, it is likely that this person will develop a fierce abandonment anxiety. As a result, this image is constantly present in his office, and the office messenger constantly sends this image to the archive, which strives to produce abandonment experiences again – which in turn reinforces the abandonment anxiety.

The cycle "image in the office → image in the archive → event matching the image → image in the office" maintains and reinforces itself: the repetition compulsion.

There is an obvious need to become aware of one's own inner images and to transform them and bring them to a higher level, thereby ending the compulsion to constantly repeat unpleasant experiences. In exploring these images, pendulums, dream journeys, etc. can help, but the actual healing is a subject beyond the scope of this book.

Practically, the repetition compulsion also exists in the case of pleasant things: one experiences something pleasant, sends the image of this situation into the archive, which then creates such a situation again: the "lucky child".

This cycle can also be experienced in meditation: If one has spoken a mantra for a while, concentrated on the kundalini, gone into silence, etc., this state begins to stabilize. It carries itself, so to speak, it calls itself forth.

At first, one experiences a threshold that one has to overcome in order to enter this state. When one has reached the state, one lies in it like in a shallow valley from which one cannot simply roll out. To get out of that state, you have to expend some energy and climb up the "slope of the valley" and then get back into another state.

This feedback effect is an important aspect of the dynamics of the office messenger.

III 7. Obsession

Obsession is the extreme case of automatic movements – it might be better to call it "loss of control over one's own body". However, obsessions are extremely rare.

When one experiences such a condition in a person, one should consider that it could also be an internal process, i.e. a violent contradiction in the psyche of the person in question, which has led to repressions, emotional outbursts, loss of reality, etc. Not every extreme action of a person is due to an obsession. The "spirit" that shows itself in a state of possession, that is, precisely in extreme and often violent behavior associated with a clouding of consciousness, can also be just a part of the psyche of the person concerned.

However, as hypnosis shows, it is possible for a person to take control of another person. Since there is also remote hypnosis, performed by telepathy, non-material beings should also be able to perform hypnosis.

The classic idea in possession is that a demon has taken control of a human being. But what is a demon? This is a question where the answer depends very much on one's worldview: a "messenger of the devil", a spirit whose nature one cannot understand, a deceased person, a natural being …

In general, one is on safe ground if one first simply says, like Socrates, "I know that I know nothing." Then one can look at what one can observe, and then describe what one sees. In a second step, one then looks for regularities and formulates them in as general a way as possible. Thereby one receives a world picture, which is completely based on one's own experiences and of which one knows that it consists of descriptions of one's own experiences.

If, on the other hand, one starts from a world view and explains the world from this world view, one is completely dependent on this world view – one's own world view stands and falls with the correctness of this world view. If one is e.g. Christian or Muslim and in the own world view therefore devils and demons occur, it is delicate to trust (or to fear) that these beings actually exist. Possibly one creates by this conception in the own psyche only pictures of devils, which work then in one's own psyche like devils …

By family constellations etc. one can, if one wants, concretely experience spirits of the dead and their work. If one has also experienced a poltergeist once, one can assume with sufficient justification that there are spirits of the dead, which can also still interfere in the lives of the living.

So if a spirit, i.e. a deceased, actually reports to a living person, it will usually do so with knocking noises, with words, sometimes also with a pulling at the bedspread and the like. Since a spirit also needs motivation for its actions, a spirit will also try to reach its goal. In most cases these will be dreams, i.e. images that the spirit sends to the sleeping living person.

What concrete advantage would a spirit have from putting a living person into a seizure-like raving, i.e. into a possession? If the spirit should be an out-and-out sadist, it could probably torture the living in a more effective way – after all, the typical unconsciousness of a possessed person is not exactly the state in which the possessed person experiences particularly much of what is happening …

All in all, it is not impossible that there is an actual possession, i.e. hypnosis by a spirit – but this possibility is not probable. In any case, it is advisable to check first whether it is an epileptic seizure, a psychosis or a schizophrenia.

Something more general can be said about obsessions: Every outer image needs an inner image to which it can connect – otherwise the outer image cannot have an effect on the person concerned. A hypnotist or a spirit who wants to make a completely serene person, resting in his own power, run amok, has a hard time, because he will not find any repressed aggression in the serene person, which he could use as a drive for the amok run.

So, for what it wants to achieve, a spirit will choose the people who already carry in themselves an inclination for something similar.

An exorcism is basically a hypnosis of the possessed by the exorcist, by which the exorcist takes control of the possessed and drives the spirit away. Subsequently, the exorcist wakes the possessed person up again from his hypnosis caused by the spirit.

This process sounds much less dramatic when described as hypnosis: The helper dissolves the hypnosis into which a person has fallen as a result of the actions of a spirit – provided it really was a "spirit-hypnosis" and not the temporary dominance of a repressed part of the psyche of the person concerned.

Exorcism is a fight between the hypnosis of the spirit and the hypnosis of the exorcist.

Generally speaking, possessions are possible, but extremely rare.

IV   The Collective Auto-Movement

As a third form besides the intentional automatic movements and the unintentional automatic movements, there are the collective automatic movements.

The intentional automatic movement occurs most frequently; the collective automatic movement is naturally the rarest – simply because it requires a group of people and not just one individual. The one exception is advertising …

These collective automatic movements all originate in the collective subconscious – they are brought about by images created (or, in the case of advertising, perceived) together by many people.

IV 1.   Advertising

The most obvious form of collective auto-movement is advertising: the images and texts and accompanying music of advertising are intended to make people buy something they would not buy without that advertising …

The automatic movements targeted are reaching for the advertised brand of cigarettes, craving the advertised type of whiskey, and buying the "best car in the world."

Advertising could also be called "neuro-pictorial programming" of people, i.e. "programming people's brains through images". This works (unfortunately) quite well.

IV 2.   Astrology

If one understands "automatic movements" very broadly, astrology also falls under this term: one can read from a birth chart how a person will behave in a certain situation, and one can see from the current position of the planets what kind of event will take place on the day in question, and so on.

The automatic movements are the behavior of people, animals, plants, weather, political situation, etc. corresponding to the position of the planets.

IV 3. Mass hypnosis

In a narrower sense, collective auto-movement is found in mass hypnosis, in the suggestive guidance of large crowds. This phenomenon is mainly found in dictatorships during propaganda and large marches, demagogic speeches and the like.

The most famous example might be Josef Göbbels sentence "Do you want total war?". It is worth reading this speech of Göbbels, which he delivered on 18.2.1943 in the Berlin Sportpalast, to see how a clever demagogic speech can be constructed.

One can argue whether "mass hypnosis" is the appropriate word for what happens in propaganda and demagogy – but the effect is the same as in hypnosis: the speaker gets his listeners to do what he wants. The result is a largely unconscious action, not decided by the speaker's own will – in other words, a collective, externally controlled auto-movement.

IV 4. Collective visions

In most religions, there are apparitions of deities that are perceived not only by a single individual, but by a large community. This could be understood as an unplanned collective dream journey – although the people perceive the deity with open eyes – the inner image overlaps the outer image.

Such processes occur with individual humans more often. These visions are impressive, but they have nothing dramatic. I myself have had several such perceptions. As long as one is aware of the fact that in these cases an inner image is superimposed on the optical perception of the world, this is no problem and does not lead to a loss of contact with reality.

These visions, since they usually originate not only from one's own psyche, but from the collective subconscious, are also not "only" images, but images that can also have an effect – such as a healing. This is just as true for Marian apparitions as for the perception of elves.

What is "automatically moved" in this case is the optical perception.

However, visions can also be of an acoustic nature – I once heard Pan playing the flute in the forest together with Axel, my magic teacher, during a Pan invocation. There were not many sounds we heard, but it was the most intense music I have heard so far.

There are also "smell visions" – they occur especially when summoning demons: you often smell sulfur. I know this from my own experience – again together with Axel.

IV 5.   Collective Telekinesis

The collective telekinesis also belongs to the collective automatic movements – even if what is moving is in most cases external objects and circumstances.

The simplest case is moving a paper spinning top. In pairs this is often easier than alone, but whether two, three or five or more people spin a paper spinning top makes no difference. So the paper spinning top is not a useful example of collective telekinesis – because no particular effect is seen when many people are involved in the experiment. The paper wheel ist not spinning faster, for example.

The "Jesus-People", who were also active in Germany around 1980 and promoted a living Christianity, used "collective telekinesis" extensively – if you want to call it that. They got together in the morning and looked at what they needed that day: e.g. food, a place to stay, money for a train ride and a bicycle. Then they prayed together to Jesus – and by the evening they had found or been given everything they needed. This procedure can also be called "Christian magic".

What is moved in the process are the "circumstances" that, by "meaningful coincidences," bring about the things and events that have been asked for. These things and events are not brought about consciously, but only invited – i.e. the office messenger is sent off.

Another phenomenon are the "weeping statues" which are reported from time to time and which are found preferably at places of pilgrimage – i.e. where many people pray intensively.

In 1985, there were reports of statues of Mary moving in 30 places in Ireland at the same time.

Similar phenomena, all of which can be counted as collective telekinesis, are reported from various religions. For example, there are reports from the Germanic tribes of statues of gods that moved their hand and released a ring after an intense prayer.

Of course, it would be delicate to simply believe these reports if one has not already experienced something of this kind with statues or at least generally with telekinesis, materializations or the like, which shows that the crying or moving statues are only variants of something that one has already experienced oneself in a small way.

In these statue phenomena, what is moved is a part of a statue. The trigger is most likely the belief of the people who worship a deity in the statues in question.

IV 6.   Crop circles

The last variant of the collective automatic movement is the crop circles. The crop circles are areas of flattened grain in mature crop fields, known since about 1920. In the beginning these were simple circular areas of a few meters in diameter – now complex patterns and graphics appear, sometimes over 100m long.

Naturally, there is a great dispute as to whether they were created by humans or not. There are four arguments that they were not created by humans, but were created in some other way – at least a part of them:

- They appear very quickly within a few hours, as has been shown by observing crop fields where crop circles appear almost every year.

- The corn stalks are bent at the knots of the stalk – so the rather rigid stalks are not uprooted and laid flat, nor are they broken at the stalk.

- The patterns are extremely complex and of an aesthetic that is otherwise not found in art.

- In a fresh crop circle even untrained people feel an intense tension and an electric tingling (as it is typical for life force phenomena). This "charge" in the crop circles is not homogeneous, but is different at each point of the crop circle pattern, and on closer inspection often coincides with the pattern itself.

V   Overview

The considerations of the auto-movement in this book can be sorted in several ways, which once again gives a clearer picture of these phenomena.

V 1.   The originator of the movement

First of all, one can investigate who initiates the auto-movement. As the causer of the movement can be considered the human being himself, another human being, a collective being or a non-physical being (deity, spirit).

The following overview shows that independent, conscious causation of automatic movement is by far the most frequent case – followed by group causation.

The foreign causation is mainly hypnosis, mass hypnosis and advertising – with advertising being very widespread.

A deity or a spirit as a causer are quite rare – the whole world as a causer, however, is constantly effective: astrology.

The causer (part 1)			
man (oneself)	**another human being**	**group**	**deity, spirit etc.**
a) conscious			
pendulum	hypnosis	dream journeys	
divining rod	remote hypnosis	vision	
finger monitor	mass hypnosis	glossolalia	
automatic writing	advertising	chair experiment	
body monitor		invocation	
automatic speaking		oracle	
body messenger		firewalk	
finger signal		power animal	
memory messenger		telekinesis	
dream travel			
inner hearing			
glossolalia			
understanding foreign languages			
smilie experiment			
dragon claw experiment			
shaolin experiment			
hepp experiment			
paper wheel experiment			
sigil magic			
wishes			
arm experiment			
invocation			
oracle			
firewalk			
power animal			

The causer (part 2)			
man (oneself)	*another human being*	*group*	*deity, spirit etc.*
b) unconscious			
sleepwalking			astrology
unconscious invocation			crop circles
stigmata			obsession
repetition compulsion			

V 2. The moved

Next, one can examine what is moved in the auto-movement: one's own body, one's own perception, the body of another person, an object or a situation – the last two cases being generally counted as magic.

Essentially, auto-movement involves moving one's own body or the body of another.

The inner perceptions are another monitor for the same process as moving one's own body.

Apart from astrology, auto-movement by something other than a human (deity, spirit) is a rare phenomenon. Only the crop circles have been established in the meantime as collective telekinesis.

The moved				
one's own body	*one's own perception*	*the body of another*	*an object*	*situations*
a) conscious				a) situation
commute	memory messenger	dragon claw experiment	paper wheel experiment	sigil magic
dowsing rod	dream journey	shaolin experiment		wünsche
wishes finger monitor	inner hearing	Hepp experiment		invokation
automatic writing	understanding foreign languages	chair experiment		repetition compulsion
body monitor	advertising	arm experiment		crop circles
automatic speech		hypnosis		
body messenger		remote hypnosis		
finger signal		collective visions		
glossolalia		collective telekinesis		
smilie experiment				
oracle				
firewalk				
power animal				
b) unconscious				b) all
sleepwalking	mass hypnosis			astrology
unconscious invocation				
stigmata				
possession				

V 3.   The awareness of the movement-intention

One can also ask how something is moved (consciously, unconsciously or collectively) – the structure of this book in three main chapters is also based on this. With "consciousness" is not meant the consciousness of the auto-movement itself, which is already unconscious by definition, but the decision to perform an auto-move-ment.

Most of the auto-movement arises from a conscious decision.

The unconscious variants almost all fall into the category of hypnosis, except for sleepwalking and stigmata – advertising is a socially-accepted form of mass hypnosis …

The two important collective unconscious forms of auto-movement are astrology and crop circles.

Awareness (part 1)			
Body parts	**Origin**		
	conscious	*unconscious*	*collective unconscious*
arm	pendulum	hypnosis	
	dowsing rod		
	smilie experiment		
	dragon claw experiment		
finger	automatic writing	Hypnosis	
	Finger monitor	Finger signal	
hands/feet		stigmata	
body	body-monitor	sleepwalking	Tears of statues etc.
	Body messenger	Hypnosis	
	Shaolin experiment	Remote hypnosis	
	Firewalk	Possession	
	Invocation	advertising	
	unconscious invocation	power animal	
	mass hypnosis		
	power animal		
tongue	glossolalia	hypnosis	glossolalia
	automatic speaking		
ears	inner hearing	hypnosis	vision
	understanding foreign languages		
eyes	dream journey	hypnosis	Vision
	vision		
intuition	memory messenger		

Awareness (part 2)			
Body parts	*Origin*		
	conscious	*unconscious*	*collective unconscious*
external things	telekinesis		crop circles
	Hepp experiment etc.		
	firewalk etc.		
	chair experiment		
	oracle		
	arm experiment		
	Tarot, I Ching etc.		
	paper wheel experiment		
situations	sigil magic		astrology
	wishes		
	repetition compulsion		

V 4. Telepathy and Telekinesis

Finally, one can also check whether the auto-movement only takes place "internally", i.e. only between the waking consciousness, the subconsciousness and the body, or whether telepathy and telekinesis also played a role in the auto-movement under consideration and consequently it is an "external" process. Some processes, such as scrying, occur in both categories because they can be performed with and without telepathy. This is true for quite a few variants of auto-movement – they have been combined into one common column in the table for clarity.

As the overview shows, almost all processes of auto-movement are either always or sometimes connected with telepathy or are connected with telekinesis. Only four experiments are certainly not related to telepathy and telekinesis.

This again shows what an important tool auto-movement is for magic.

internal and external auto-movement		
internal auto-movement	**external auto-movement**	
	telepathy	*telekinesis*
memory messenger	divining rod	dragon claw experiment
smilie experiment	understanding foreign languages	shaolin experiment
sleepwalking	oracle	Hepp experiment
advertising	power animal	chair experiment
	remote hypnosis	paper wheel experiment
	obsession	sigil magic
pendulum		wishes
finger monitor		arm experiment
automatic writing		firewalk
body monitor		stigmata
automatic speaking		astrology
body messenger		crop circles
finger signal		
dream journeys		
inner listening		
glossolalia		
invocation		
unconscious invocation		
repetition compulsion		
hypnosis		
mass hypnosis		
visions		

English Books by Harry Eilenstein

- Living Magic (261 p.)	- Mandalas for Beginners
- The Synthesis of Physics and Magic (192 p.)	- Money Magic for Beginners
- Astral Projection for Beginners (60 p.)	- Love Magic for Beginners
- Invocations for Beginners (52 p.)	- Magic Research for Beginners
- Evocations for Beginners (62 p.)	- Self-awareness for Beginners
- Auto-Movement for Beginners (60 p.)	- Symbolism of Numbers for Beginners
- Elves for Beginners (56 p.)	- Language of the Moon – for Beginners
These books will be puplished soon:	- Magic Chant for Beginners
- Telepathy for Beginners	- Prophecy for Beginners
- Telepathy for Advanced Learners	- Shamanism for Beginners
- Telekinesis for Beginners	- Magic Objects for Beginners
- Life Force for Beginners	- Da'ath-Magic for Beginners
- Meditation for Beginners	- Crop Circles for Beginners
- Kundalini for Beginners	- Feng Shui for Beginners
- Hypnosis for Beginners	- Magic for Beginners – Anthology I
- Chakra-Magic for Beginners	- Magic for Beginners – Anthology II
- Astrology for Beginners	- Magic for Beginners – Anthology III
- Ritual Magic for Beginners	- Magic for Beginners – Anthology IV

Bücher von Harry Eilenstein

Religion allgemein	**Germanen**
- Die sieben Schritte des Lebens (428 S.)	- Die Götter der Germanen (87 Bände – siehe
- Muttergöttin und Schamanen (168 S.)	nächste Seite)
- Göbekli Tepe (472 S.)	- Odin (300 S.)
- Die Göttin von Göbekli Tepe (144 S.)	**Kelten**
- Totempfähle (440 S.)	- Cernunnos (690 S.)
- Christus (60 S.)	- Taliesin (228 S.)
- Dakini (80 S.)	- Der Kessel von Gundestrup (220 S.)
- Vajra (76 S.)	- Der Chiemsee-Kessel (76)
Ägypten	**Psychologie**
- Hathor und Re 1: Götter und Mythen im	- Über die Freude (100 S.)
Alten Ägypten (432 S.)	- Das Geheimnis des inneren Friedens (252 S.)
- Hathor und Re 2: Die altägyptische Religion –	- Das Beziehungsmandala (52 S.)
Ursprünge, Kult und Magie (396 S.)	- Gefühle und ihre Verwandlungen (404 S.)
- Isis (508 S.)	- einsgerichtet (140 S.)
Indogermanen	- Liebe und Eigenständigkeit (216 S.)
- Die Entwicklung der indogermanischen	- Von innerer Fülle zu äußerem Gedeihen (52 S.)
Religionen (700 S.)	**Heilung**
- Wurzeln und Zweige der indogermanischen	- Die Symbolik der Krankheiten (76 S.)
Religion (224 S.)	**Kunst**
	- Herz des Tanzes – Tanz des Herzens (160 S.)
	Drama
	- König Athelstan (104 S.)

Bücher von Harry Eilenstein

„Magie für Anfänger"

- Telepathie für Anfänger (60 S.)
- Telepathie für Fortgeschrittene (52 S.)
- Telekinese für Anfänger (52 S.)
- Lebenskraft für Anfänger (60 S.)
- Meditation für Anfänger (56 S.)
- Kundalini für Anfänger (100 S.)
- Hypnose für Anfänger (56 S.)
- Auto-Movement für Anfänger (56 S.)
- Chakra-Magie für Anfänger (148 S.)
- Astralreisen für Anfänger (56 S.)
- Astrologie für Anfänger (120 S.)
- Ritual-Magie für Anfänger (56 S.)
- Mandalas für Anfänger (68 S.)
- Geldzauber für Anfänger (56 S.)
- Liebeszauber für Anfänger (52 S.)
- Invokationen für Anfänger (52 S.)
- Evokationen für Anfänger (60 S.)
- Elfen für Anfänger (56 S.)
- Magie-Forschung für Anfänger (140 S.)
- Selbsterkenntnis für Anfänger (52 S.)
- Zahlensymbolik für Anfänger (60 S.)
- Die Sprache des Mondes – für Anfänger (116 S.)
- Zaubergesänge für Anfänger (100 S.)
- Zukunftschau für Anfänger (60 S.)
- Schamanismus für Anfänger (52 S.)
- Magische Gegenstände für Anfänger (68 S.)
- Da'ath-Magie für Anfänger (64 S.)
- Kornkreise für Anfänger (348 S.)
- Feng Shui für Anfänger (96 S.)
- Magie für Anfänger – Sammelband I (696 S.)
- Magie für Anfänger – Sammelband II (664 S.)
- Magie für Anfänger – Sammelband III (580 S.)

„Traumreisen"

- Traumreisen zu Heilpflanzen (700 S.)

Magie

- Handbuch für Zauberlehrlinge (408 S.)
- Tarot (104 S.)
- Physik und Magie (184 S.)
- Die Synthese von Physik und Magie (200S.)
- Die Magie-Formel (156 S.)
- Krafttiere – Tiergöttinnen – Tiertänze (112 S.)
- Schwitzhütten (524 S.)
- Mythen und Magie der Harfe (116 S.)
- Magie heute – Berichte aus der Praxis (288 S.)

Meditation

- Der Lebenskraftkörper (230 S.)
- Die Chakren (100 S.)
- Das Chakren-System mit den Nebenchakren (296 S.)
- Organe und Chakren (64 S.)
- Die platonischen Körper in den Chakren (156 S.)
- Meditation (140 S.)
- Drachenfeuer (124 S.)
- Kundalini I (676 S.)
- Reinkarnation (156 S.)
- einsgerichtet (140 S.)

Astrologie

- Astrologie (496 S.)
- Photo-Astrologie (428 S.)
- Die astrologischen Aspekte (88 S.)
- Horoskop und Seele (120 S.)

Kabbala

- Kursus der praktischen Kabbala (150 S.)
- Eltern der Erde (450 S.)
- Blüten des Lebensbaumes:
    - Die Struktur des kabbalistischen Lebensbaumes (370 S.)
    - Der kabbalistische Lebensbaum als Forschungshilfsmittel (580 S.)
    - Der kabbalistische Lebensbaum als spirituelle Landkarte (520 S.)

Die Themen der 87 Bände der Reihe „Die Götter der Germanen"